Jeanne... the Angel Who Saved Me

David Sieben

For publishing inquiries, contact:

Lisa Pelto

c/o CMI

4822 South 133rd Street

Omaha, NE 68137

Color Paperback ISBN: 978-1-936840-49-6

Black & White Paperback ISBN: 978-1-936840-48-9

Library of Congress Cataloging data on file with the publisher

Printed in the USA

10 9 8 7 6 5 4 3 2 1

To laugh often and much;
to win the respect of intelligent people
and the affection of children,
to leave the world and better place,
to even know one life has breathed easier
because you have lived,
this is to have succeeded.

~Emerson

Prologue

My childhood memories come back to haunt me regularly. When I am alone, I try to think of the good things in my life. I remember the people who were kind to me when I was going through difficult times. Without them, I don't think I would have made it. For many years I dwelled on negatives. I thought about the hard times I was living through.

When the love of my life went to heaven, I felt abandoned like I had been as a child. I lost the one person who taught me to be happy. She was my teacher, my lover, and my spiritual advisor. When I was lost, she helped me to find the way. When she left this earth, I was on a journey without a compass.

Over the past few months, I believe I have rediscovered the path to happiness. With the help of some very kind and compassionate people, I have found my way and I am beginning to experience the happiness that I had for 64 years with my Jeanne.

Jeanne, the Angel Who Saved Me

Chapter 1

The Beginning Years

I was born November 29, 1927, during the last years of Prohibition. My memories begin at five years old. It was then that I became aware there was no adult male in our family. No one ever talked about it and we were shushed when anyone asked why we didn't have a dad like some of our playmates. I was too young to remember my father. His name was Oswald. He was in the U.S. Army and fought in France during the last year of World War I.

After the war, my father had a difficult time adjusting. He became involved with people who bootlegged liquor and moonshine. According to relatives who lived at the time, my father went missing in 1931 when the car he had been driving the day before was found abandoned at a gravel pit. The sheriff along with state and federal police all investigated and said there was no information that could explain what happened to my father. His fate remains unknown to this day. He was declared "missing" and his Army uniform continued to hang in a closet for years. My mother kept it handy just in case he came back. He never did.

In 1917, my father married my mother, Susan Unger, before he went overseas. My parents had ten children. I was the seventh. The third child, a son, died of pneumonia at 18 months old. A baby boy born ten months after me died at birth. My brother, Norman, born in 1919, was only twelve years old when our father disappeared. He became responsible for looking after seven siblings.

When Norman got the opportunity to work on Hobby Farm for the CEO of Pillsbury Mills, he moved hundreds of miles away. Born a year after Norman, my brother Gene joined the Navy when Pearl Harbor was attacked and was gone until 1946. My brother Jimmy also left home to work for room and board when he was 12 years old. I was then the oldest of the remaining children.

In our family each of us was responsible for watching over the brother or sister who was next in line. For me, that was my brother Donny. Donny was responsible for watching over the next youngest to him, Patty, who had never seen our father before he disappeared.

Of all the memories of our childhood, one vividly sticks in my mind. On Donny's first day of grade school, a train hit a cattle truck. There were animals lying all over the tracks with broken legs. The police walked up and down the line with revolvers, shooting each cow in the head. I had nightmares for years to come.

The 1930s were difficult for us. We lived in a small house just outside of Sauk Centre, Minnesota. Sauk Centre is known as the birthplace of the novelist Sinclair Lewis who used the town as inspiration for his novel, "Main Street."

My mother married Rudolf Sukke when she realized that my father was never coming back. They had a baby daughter and named her Helen. Mother had a difficult time with postpartum depression and couldn't make herself get out of bed. She was unable to take care of us.

Because it became increasingly difficult to live with my mother, Rudolf moved out of the house and into a place a mile away from us, leaving us on our own.

My sister, Lorraine, two years older than I, also had a difficult time getting along with our mother. She moved in with her boyfriend's mother, leaving four of us behind. We remaining siblings lived together at the farm for about five years until my brother Donny was picked up by our father's brother, Uncle

Bill, and raised as his own son. I was disappointed. I was the next in line and thought I should have been the one to have this opportunity. I didn't see Donny again until he graduated from high school.

I was now in charge of my two younger sisters, Patty and Helen.

When we first moved onto the Sukke farm, there was no road. We had only a trail through the woods. A couple years later we had a gravel road and a telephone. There was an outhouse out back. All summer long I would collect wood and pile it beside the house for the upcoming winter. We had a fire going all the time, even during the summer when we needed a cookstove to cook our meals. We used kerosene lanterns for light. We eventually installed a gas generator to charge up a series of batteries enabling us to have electricity. This allowed us to listen to the radio and stay up after dark.

For the seven years I lived on the farm I learned life skills through the school of necessity. I started the fires. I cooked oatmeal, corn meal, and fried potatoes, and baked bread for our meals. I fed the chickens. I helped to build structures from the ground up, do cement work, put up rafters and roofs, and take care of our farm animals. Those years were hard, but we always had enough to eat. Being five miles from town with no vehicle, we were pretty isolated. If I wanted to go anywhere, I had to walk over to the closest neighbor and ask if they were going to town. If they were, they would allow me to ride along. That was the only way I got to do anything on Saturday nights.

When I was in 8th grade, I had to walk a mile to a one-room schoolhouse. This was never a hardship for me because I really liked school. My teacher only had an 8th grade education, so she wasn't able to offer me much outside of the basic reading, writing and arithmetic. I wanted more. I want to learn everything I could about the world outside of Sauk Centre. Our school only carried one textbook for the year and I didn't have access to other books. I wanted to have a book with me all the time. If I needed something new to read, I had to ask someone to go to the library in town and borrow books for me. One of these that I remember was a book by Ernest Hemingway. It was the best novel I had ever read.

During this period of my life I got very sick. I was diagnosed with rheumatic fever. The doctor prescribed sulfa drugs, told me to stay in bed and drink lots of water. Our water supply was a well with a pump located halfway down a hill. I couldn't walk that far so my siblings had to go to the well to bring back buckets of water. My kidneys were failing. I wasn't sure I was going to survive. With lots of prayer and gallons of water I got through it.

My sickness lasted from March until that winter. I missed part of the 8th grade and the first part of the 9th. I started 9th grade in November and by Christmas, I had caught up to the rest of the class.

CHAPTER 2

School Years

When I was to start my senior year in high school in 1944, I drove a car and delivered eggs and cream before class. I played saxophone in the school band, learning all the big band songs that were popular in the mid-forties. I got pretty good on the saxophone. I was given a sax solo for the school band concert but I ended up not going. I couldn't attend because I was sick. This was a huge disappointment for me.

I became aware of two girls in the band that played the drums. I had missed my opportunity to shine in front of them and I never had the nerve to speak to the girls. One day one of them came to me and said her friend had noticed me and had been talking about me. She said this friend was really interested in me and I should meet her on the street where she always walked. So I did. When I said hello to the girl, I didn't get the response I expected. She tore into me and said, "Don't bother me again." She told me that she knew who had put me up to this. This was my first experience with fickle teenage girls. I didn't know what to think.

On New Year's Day 1945 during one of the coldest winters of the 20th century, the sheriff came out to our farmhouse. He said he was taking my two younger sisters, Patty and Helen, and me to a house my mother had inherited from her father. We were to stay there until our mother was released from the state mental hospital. At that time there was a belief in the mental health community that they had found a cure for manic depression. Patients were released from the hospital and sent home. When they started to get their symptoms back, they returned to the hospital and continued treatment. Some of them returned to the hospital in worse condition than before. My mother stayed with us for a very brief time before her conditions worsened and she had to go back.

When the sheriff arrived to move us to our mother's house, I warned him that it was a mistake. It wouldn't turn out well. He said he was following orders, which were to take us to the house and no more. From the first day, we had problems.

From January through May, my sisters and I lived in primitive conditions. The house was not ready for winter. It was cold and drafty. We never had enough fuel to heat the house. There was no food and no money. Every day I walked to the bakery in town and asked the owner if she had any rolls or doughnuts that were damaged or too old to sell. If she would save some for me, I would stop by after school to pick them up. This kind lady gave me enough to keep us going another day. We lived on baked goods for five months until we were picked up by authorities and sent to different places.

My stepfather, Rudolph Sukke, heard that we were living in bad conditions. He wanted to get his own daughter, Helen, out of there. He picked up my little sister when she was five years old. He had remarried after divorcing my mother. He and his second wife provided a home for Helen. Mother accused him of kidnapping their daughter, but after numerous court appearances the court awarded legal custody to the Sukkes. I didn't see Helen for the next thirty years.

Me in 1943

Jeanne, the Angel Who Saved Me

CHAPTER 3

Too Sick to Walk

All through my high school years, I never had a time when there was any structure to my life. I was always afraid that I could be uprooted at any time and taken away by someone who didn't know me and placed in a strange place with people I didn't know. I changed homes four times when I was 16 years old.

In high school I became sick once again. I was not concentrating in class and at times I would fall asleep at my desk. My teachers noticed, but did nothing to help. They attributed it to my own misbehavior. The principal asked if there was something going on at home that he should be aware of, but I didn't want to bring our situation to anyone's attention. I didn't trust the system.

When I missed two weeks of school, one of my classmates walked out to the farm. He asked me what was wrong, and why I wasn't coming to school. I told him that I couldn't walk and had had a sore throat for a long time. I was losing weight. I was 6 foot tall and weighed 120 pounds soaking wet. I imagined I looked like the inmates of the German concentration camps in the last year of World War II.

My friend was concerned when he saw my condition. He promised that he would talk to his father who was the minister of one of the protestant churches in town and would come back to see me within a couple days. Shortly afterward, a friend of my classmate's father, an army doctor from Fort Snelling in Minneapolis, showed up to check me over. The doctor found that I was severely malnourished. My sore throat had affected my heart and the valves were being damaged. I had rheumatic fever for the second time. I needed penicillin, three meals a day, and bed-rest.

This was the first time anybody had ever visited me at any place I lived. I asked my friend if he would bring me my schoolbooks so I could keep up with the class. I had all day to read and I wanted to take final exams. I asked my friend to get permission from the school to act as my proctor. I was eventually able to take my exams which I passed.

During my illness the girl from the school band came out to visit me. Before I was confident that I had rheumatic fever I warned her I might be contagious. At this time we were in a polio epidemic. I had several of the symptoms and if I had polio, it would be dangerous for her to be around me. She still came to see me every day. It was one of the kindest things that anyone had done for me. I wasn't sure of her feelings for me. Was she just being a friend or was it more? I told her that I had no control over my life. I could be taken away at any time and there was no future for us together.

Even though it took a superhuman effort, I walked the girl home. We talked until her mother came home from work. Her mother was the lady at the bakery who had given me the baked goods that my sisters and I had lived off of for months. I wanted her to know how much I appreciated what she had done for me. Her kindness had kept us from starving. I believed she saved us. I was also happy she let her daughter come to see me. She was the first girl who had ever showed interest in me. I learned a lesson from these two people. They say that the apple never falls far from the tree. It was true of them. This kind mother had taught her daughter to be caring just like her.

For five months, my sister Patty and I lived together. I had been thankful that up until this point, no one ever asked how bad my situation had become. But now we needed help. The doctor who had checked me over stopped at the courthouse and informed the people there that something terrible was happening in their county. It had gotten to a critical state. The doctor said I didn't have more than a few days left to live if something wasn't done.

The next day the county health services and child welfare workers drove up. They told me that they would be back in two hours and I should pack up my stuff in the meantime. When they come back, I didn't have anything packed. I didn't have anything but what I was wearing. Before the day was over someone dropped off a box of clothes for me at the house. These were the first new clothes I ever had and they were going to have to last me until I made my own money.

County officials told me that Patty and I would be driven to St Cloud, Minnesota 50 miles away. They were taking Patty, who was 12 years old, to a foster home where there were babies to take care of. Patty was moved each year to a different home. She told me once that the last foster mother was the best one she ever had. She was finally a part of a family. That was my dream since I could remember.

As for me, I was supposed to go to an orphanage where there would be plenty of kids to be with, but I was sadly disappointed.

Jeanne, the Angel Who Saved Me

CHAPTER 4

Prison Without Walls

Because the doctor who had examined me said he couldn't be sure if I was contagious and that I was too sick to be around other kids, the orphanage was out. Instead I was taken to the Old Folks Home. I was given my own room with a flushing toilet and a bathtub. I got three meals a day. I had medical care with daily shots of Penicillin. This was the start of my journey back to health. My weight climbed from 125 pounds to about 140 in the nine months I stayed there.

However, my life there was not without problems. I was confined to my one small room. I could not visit with anyone until they were sure I was no longer contagious. My only possibility of a friend was the case worker from social services. She was kind. I really liked her. I thought I could talk to her about anything bothering me. The only other person I saw was the nurse who popped in to give me shots of Penicillin. I was young. I was alone. I was lonely.

The Old Folks Home was a block from the river. As I got better I had a hard time staying inside. It was May. The sun was shining. I wanted to be outdoors. I wanted to explore along the riverbank. So, after breakfast I would go out the back door, returning shortly before lunch.

That summer two people drowned in the river. Officials closed the swimming beach. The city pool was closed because two kids had contracted polio. St. Cloud had granite quarries where the usable rock had been mined and the holes had filled with water. Kids would go out to the old quarries to swim. In 1945 there were ninety-two quarry holes around the city. I sometimes hiked out to the nearest one and swam.

One day when I was a few blocks from the Old Folks Home, I thought I heard my name being called. I stopped and looked around. I saw a young girl running toward me. She kept calling. As she got closer I recognized my sister Patty. We hadn't seen each other since the day we were taken away in separate cars to go to different homes. We had lived within a few blocks of each other for four months and nobody told us. I was happy to see my sister. I now had a place to go on my walks.

I thought I was getting along fine and could do this all summer. But, I was getting too independent for the people who watched over me. When they found out I was leaving the home and exploring, I was told I couldn't go anywhere by myself. I had to get permission every time I wanted to leave. They had complete control over me. The people who ran the Old Folks Home also ran the county jail. I had difficulty with a number of their rules and conditions. The rules were too restrictive and I was having trouble holding onto my sanity. For 16 years I never had any rules to live by. I always made decisions for myself and my younger siblings. So, I found new ways to spend my time and new places to go where I could meet other people and talk things over.

County officials ordered me to report to the courthouse and tell them what I remembered of my life with mother. I told them I didn't remember anything. They thought I was lying because I knew they were trying to make a case to keep my mother locked away in a mental institution. They warned me that if I got into trouble, I would be hauled away to the orphanage. They said that like it was a terrible place to end up. It would have been a blessing. The orphanage would have been a much better place for me to spend my teen years. At least I would have been with other kids. At least I could have had friends.

One day a care giver told me there was a man outside the Old Folks Home who wanted to see me. The man was my father's brother, Uncle Bill. Uncle Bill told me he had been appointed by the court as my guardian. I asked him what that meant. I was curious how that would affect my life. He just said that the people who saw me every day were reporting my escapades. I wasn't following the rules. Those who were supposed to be looking after me were frustrated by my behavior. My new guardian told me that I would have plenty of rules to live by while I was under the care of the county. There wasn't much said about how the guardianship would benefit me.

When someone would ask me what I wanted to do with my life, I would say, "I want to go to school." I want to do something worthwhile with my time. If I had something to read, I could catch up with news and the great novels that were being written about the war. Whenever someone was available they borrowed library books for me. When I was able to go myself, I read medical books at the library. I learned a lot of things related to health, but especially about mental illness. Maybe I was fascinated with the treatment of mental illness because of my mother and her struggles. There was a veterans' hospital close to the Old Folks Home. Sometimes when I could get away, I would go there and visit with soldiers who were having a hard time making the change from war to civilian life. I thought in some way I could help.

I repeated my desire to go to school so many times that someone finally listened. One day someone from the sheriff's department, the care givers at the Old Folks Home, and the education officials from the State Capitol met with me to discuss my options. There were two higher education schools nearby. St. John's University produced priests. Four of my cousins and an uncle were priests. There also was a teacher's college where you could learn be a teacher. Unfortunately, I was told there was no money available to send me to college.

I did two days of tests to find out what I was good at. My hands were not flexible enough to work with small parts like watchmaking. I wasn't strong enough for manual labor. They found an opportunity for me to work with a couple of eye doctors. In the back room of the medical arts building where the doctors' prescriptions were processed, I learned a trade that would be my life's work. I settled down to a daily routine learning the metric system, diopters, prisms, astigmatism, near and far sightedness, and how to read a doctor's prescription and apply it to mechanical means to make lenses. It wasn't exactly my idea of what I wanted to do. But it was something that was available to me.

The plan was to give me a skill that would make me independent and self-sufficient. I tried to comply with the new arrangements. But it was all work and no play. One day I was invited to go to a roller skating rink. It sounded fun, so I asked permission to go. The request had to be approved through a few agencies and the answer was "no." The internship at the optical shop did not pay. I never had a dollar to spend so I had to do things that didn't cost money. I found a few places downtown where teenagers would gather to talk, drink Coke and play pool. There were many young people having problems and I wanted to do something about it. Just being there seemed to help them cope. Listening to troubled kids helped me, too. For a while this made my life bearable, but it didn't last. County officials put a stop to that too. They noticed my newfound independence and demanded again that I get their permission before leaving the Old Folks Home.

Across the street from where Patty was living was a girl named Donna. I went over to see her every day that I could slip out. We decided to go to a movie together. The movie cost 15 cents, which was all I had to my name. This was my first date and would be a one-time thing unless I found a way to earn some money. Next door to the Old Folks Home was an apartment house. I talked to the manager who let me work around the building, washing windows and scrubbing floors to make a little spending money. I worked hard and managed to make enough to take Donna to a movie every week. I found other places where I could meet young people and dance. I made new friends.

Meanwhile, social workers convinced me that talking about my life would make it better. I thought someone was finally going to listen to me. Instead they told the staff at the Old Folks Home that I was unhappy and unappreciative of everything being done for me. This became one of biggest lies and betrayals that I had to live through.

One cold day in December I called a cab and left this place forever. I had lived in this place for nine months. In my memory, this was a "Prison Without Walls."

Jerry and me in 1946

Jeanne, the Angel Who Saved Me

CHAPTER 5

Jerry and the Orphanage

A few days before Christmas of 1945 when I left the Old Folks Home, I prayed I would find a place to live before I froze to death. I met a guy named Jerry while walking around the west St. Cloud neighborhood. Jerry was living with his father. His mother had died on the 4th of July. Soon afterward, his father received notice that his fourth son was killed in the war. Four of Jerry's brothers had been in the military and all were killed. The mother, they said, died of a broken heart. His dad shut himself up in his room and rarely came out. The four youngest children were put in the orphanage. Jerry and I became very close friends.

I often went to the orphanage with Jerry to visit his brothers and sisters. Jerry and I gathered up a group of children and organized games for them to play. Of the 120 children in the orphanage, many were not able to socialize or play with others. The kids were happy that someone would come to see them. These kids had nothing. Many of them had never known the comfort of a mother's arms. Some of them had never known the meaning of friendship. They had never heard the word "love." I wanted to help, but I was in the same situation and had nothing more to offer. I told myself that if I ever grew to adulthood, I would help children like these.

Teenagers typically hung out in pool halls in those days. I used to hang out with them and listen until social workers put a stop to it. I had issues just like they did. I knew it was easier to get through the day if you could share your life with someone else and not have to worry about it being repeated. Jerry was that friend for me. I wanted to be that friend to these teens.

Jerry had a friend named Marge. We often went to her house and visited with her family. Marge had a sister, Elizabeth, who was two years older. Elizabeth was in a wheelchair, paralyzed from polio the year before. She was confined to the house without someone to push her chair. Every night the four of us walked around the neighborhood. I pushed her wheelchair and felt good that I could do something for someone and expect nothing in return.

Elizabeth and I talked about what was going on in the world and some of the things that I was experiencing at the time. After awhile she told me it wasn't fair that I was spending my time looking after her needs. She thought I should find a healthy person to be with. I told her that I enjoyed being around someone I could wait on. Besides, she was pleasant to talk with and easy on the eyes.

Jerry and I moved in together until Social Services found out. They told me that I couldn't pick the place where I wanted to live. I had to stay where I was placed by the county until I was old enough to care for myself. They didn't approve of me living with Jerry, so they placed me in a home with an unmarried Polish woman who worked for the county taking care of unwanted babies.

CHAPTER 6

Imperfect and Unwanted

When imperfect babies were born at that time, their mothers could sign away all rights. These babies were malformed, disabled, or too small to live. They would be taken away by the county and placed in a home where they would die from neglect. They were put in a back room and never fed .

After I was forbidden to live with my friend Jerry, I moved in with an unmarried Polish lady who was paid to house these unwanted babies. I used to slip into the nursery and try to make contact with them. I was discovered one day and told to never go in there again because I was interfering with the process. There was no effort to prolong the baby's short life. There was no hope given. I wasn't comfortable being a teenager caught between helpless babies and an adult who gave very little care and comfort to the children under her roof.

The Polish lady sat me down one day and told me that because I was from a German background, some people might not like me. It was the last year of the war. People were hearing about the concentration camps where unwanted groups of people were being put to death. I could not reconcile this with my religious training that taught me that all living things had right to life. Babies are unwanted. Certain ethnic groups are unwanted. Who gets to decide who is wanted and who is not?

My Polish landlady provided me with two meals a day: breakfast and supper. I was 16 years old, a growing boy. I needed more than two meals a day. Instead of going to school, I was working in the medical center optical department. I was learning what I could about the business so I could support myself when I was out on my own, but it was considered an unpaid internship. I asked the doctors if I could have a dollar a day for lunch. They gave me the money and I got to know the lady at the lunch counter in the drug store across the street. She filled a plate for me and charged me a quarter. I will add this lady to my short list of people who were kind to me when I was going through a difficult time.

After four months, I left. I left the Polish lady who was paid to NOT care for unwanted babies. She didn't seem to care that I was leaving, either. I left the medical center and my job with the eye doctors. I had the opportunity to go with a carload of people to Seattle and I took that chance. If nothing else, it would be a good way for me to see something of the world. I said goodbye to Patty, and left early the next morning.

On the way west the guys I was traveling with told me we were going to sell magazines along the way. The guy in charge dropped us off in neighborhoods in the mornings and picked us up at noon. We did the same thing in the afternoons. I was not cut out to be a good salesman. Every time we met for breakfast, lunch or dinner we got lessons in salesmanship. They taught us how to sell something that people didn't want and couldn't afford. The older salesmen were successful in conning people into buying the magazines, but we younger ones didn't do so well. I barely made enough to cover my living expenses.

I became buddies with another guy my age. We decided to go back to St. Cloud. When we approached our boss to tell him we were quitting, he lectured us. He knew it was difficult at first, he said, but claimed it got easier the more we learned about sales.

We left Fargo, North Dakota and drove west to Bismarck. After another few days with minimal results, we decided again to leave the group and head back to St. Cloud. We told the boss we had made up our minds. We were not cut out to be salesmen. At the hotel that night my new buddy was told he couldn't leave. He owed money and had to stay long enough to pay it all back. For me, I was even with my account, and I was free to go. But the boss told me something surprising. The night I had met up with the group at a hotel in St. Cloud and called Patty, she had called the sheriff. He checked out the group to see if they were crooks. The county agreed to let me go away and try to make it on my own.

I had just enough money to bus back to St. Cloud. When I returned, I went to my former job at the optical shop in the medical center. I told them I wanted my job and they took me back. I then went to the Polish lady and asked to rent my room again. I apologized for leaving on such short notice. I wanted to make a fresh start. She informed me that while I was gone, she had rented out my room to a student from St John's University. There was no room for me.

Jeanne, the Angel Who Saved Me

CHAPTER 7

Answers to Prayer

Feeling hopeless and lost I went to St. Anthony's Church with my friend Raymond Bares. I wanted to ask God to show me the way. While deep in prayer, I heard beautiful music. The choir was practicing for Novena coming up the next week. I asked the director if I could sing with the choir. He welcomed me and I felt right at home with the group. I felt I had found something I'd always wanted and needed in my me.

When I left St. Anthony's Church, I returned to see my former landlady. She had had a change of heart and told me to go have a look at the attic. Entry to the attic was by trapdoor in the ceiling in the corner of the living room. There was a pull-down ladder. She told me that if I thought I could live up there, I was welcome. The room was one big unfinished space. I could see light from the outside through the cracks in the exterior walls. There were 2 x 4's making up the floor. I had to step from one board to another to get to the cot. There was a single hanging light bulb. It was May, so it was livable, but I could see my breath in the mornings. The bathroom was located on the main level and the landlady didn't want me walking around the house during the night. I couldn't get up to go to the bathroom. It was uncomfortable waiting until morning.

After a week of choir practice, Novena started. I saw the most beautiful girl sitting just five feet away from me in the first pew. I had met her just once. She was the cousin of a girl named Laverne who lived with her grandmother across the street from the church. I often stopped to visit when going to church. We met every evening outside the house. One day she told me that she was babysitting next door at the neighbors' house. They were going away for the weekend and she was having her cousin over to help with the children. She asked if I wanted to come over to meet her. I went to the house that Saturday night. When I met Jeanne, I couldn't believe my eyes. She was slim, blonde, and blue-eyed. I prayed, "God, please let me have this person the rest of my life and I will never be a problem to anyone again!"

After the initial shock, I started to talk to her and we got along as if we had known each other our whole lives. That night we talked until the wee hours of the morning. I didn't want the night to end. But the girls had to get some sleep and I had to walk the five blocks back to where I lived. I told Jeanne I wanted to see her again, but she didn't know when she would be free. Laverne told me that Jeanne walked from 22nd Street down 3rd Street to their grandmother's house every night at about the same time I walked to church for choir practice. I made it a habit to walk down 3rd Street to meet Jeanne. She would go to her grandmother's house and I would go on to choir practice.

Novena lasted for nine days and were the best days of my life. For the following four months, Jeanne and I walked around the neighborhood holding hands. I felt blessed that I was with this beautiful girl who came from a normal family. I believed that God was walking with me all the while I was walking with Jeanne. She always made me feel that I belonged. There was no other world for us when we were together. I thanked God every day for giving us this time.

One day when I was taking my lunch break I saw something I couldn't believe. I ran outside and said, "Jeanne. What are you doing here?" She said she worked at Chef's Cafe, the coffee shop on the first floor of the medical center where I worked. I made plans to be outside when she walked by.

Everyone walked in those days. We shopped and went to church. I had just met Jeanne and we met at church every night. We spent two hours walking and holding hands. Jeanne explained to me what she had learned from the nuns in the Parochial School. We could only hold hands and share one goodnight kiss. This was to be the rule until we were married.

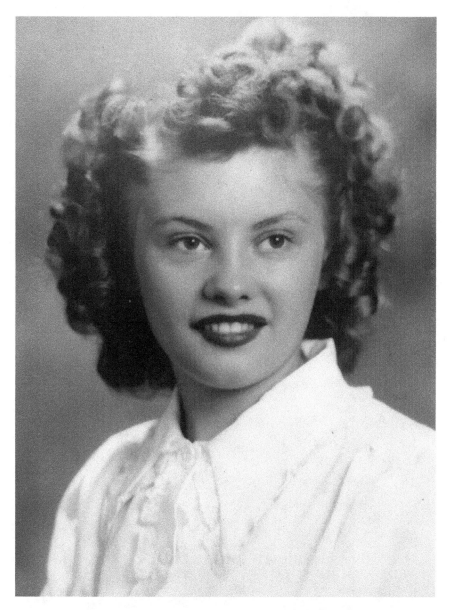

Jeanne, the most beautiful girl in the world

Jeanne, the Angel Who Saved Me

CHAPTER 8

Room for One More

Soon after I moved into the attic, the Polish Lady changed her mind again. The county had withdrawn its financial support. They were no longer paying my landlady to take care of me. I was about to become homeless and destitute. I was abandoned.

Every day I went to my friend Raymond's house. At supper time, his mother, Mrs. Bares, called her children in to eat. When I was there, she invited me to eat with the family. After a few days, she asked me why I was at their house so often during supper time. Did I not have a home to go to? I told her I didn't. I had been sleeping in an attic. She asked if there was someone she could talk to about making a home for me. I told her the county had cut all ties with me. I was alone to make it on my own. Mrs. Bares invited me to come and live with her family. There were eight children there, but she found room for one more.

There wasn't much to move from the attic room where I was staying. I had only one change of clothing. I was welcomed into the Bares family.

When Jeanne asked me where I was staying, I told her I was living with the Bares family. This turned out to be a problem for us. Jeanne told me that everyone in the neighborhood thought that the Bares family was really poor and had enough trouble with their own eight children. Her mother didn't feel I should be burdening the Bares family with one more mouth to feed. I told Jeanne this was the best home I had ever had and that I fit in perfectly. I was happy with the Bares family.

Mrs. Bares showed me a letter from the state capitol in St. Paul. I had been made a Ward of the State. I didn't know exactly what this meant, but I was allowed to stay with the Bares family until my brother, Gene, came home from the war.

Raymond Bares (on the left)

Jeanne, the Angel Who Saved Me

CHAPTER 9

Gene and Jeanne

When Gene was discharged from the Navy, he came back to live in St. Cloud. We were going to get an apartment together, so we looked for a place to live. We rented an apartment on 4th Avenue South. Gene found a job working on the pipeline coming up north from Texas. At first he had to drive about ten miles, but as the line inched further north, that distance got shorter. He bought a car with his military pay that he had saved up during his four year enlistment in the Navy. Gene had been stationed in the South Pacific supplying ships, which allowed him little to no leave in port where he could spend money.

I was excited about Gene having a car. I told my buddies we had a car we could use. If we had dates, Gene would let us borrow it. One winter day, Jeanne's friend Janet called me and said that she and Jeanne would be free on Sunday all day. I called a couple of buddies and we rode around with the girls. We played in the snow and skied behind the car. I remember Jeanne wore a Teddy Bear coat. This was the first time that Jeanne and 1 sat together in a car. We took photos with the camera I had just bought for 25 cents. I still have some of those photos. They are precious reminders.

Janet agreed to call me whenever Jeanne had time off and we could be together. Jeanne still stuck to her rule about not calling me, so I had to rely on Janet and Jeanne's cousin Laverne to let me know when she was available. We got together about twice a week. I always borrowed Gene's car and we would have a few hours to call our own.

Jeanne's 15th birthday was coming up and I wanted to give her something, but I had no money. A girl I had met before

Jeanne asked me one day if I would sing a song to her mother. She told me the name of the song and I said yes, I knew it. I told the girl to bring her mother the following day at noon to the lobby of the medical center where I worked, I would sing to her then. The next day the girl and her mother came to the lobby where I usually ate my lunch. The lady was dressed up in very colorful clothes like she was going to a party. I started to sing "Gypsy" a popular song of the 40s. By the time I was done, a crowd had gathered and clapped. The lady reached into her purse, took out a dollar bill and gave it to me. J now had the money· 1 needed to buy Jeanne's birthday present.

I shopped in jewelry stores and found a gold heart locket. I put my picture in it and gave this to Jeanne. She was really proud of her new necklace, but when she wore it home, everything changed. Jeanne didn't come to church any more, and didn't go to visit her grandmother. After a few days had passed and I didn't see Jeanne, I called her house. Her big brother told me that her mother didn't want her talking to me anymore and I wasn't to come around the house. I wasn't welcome. Family was very important to them. They didn't know me. I had no mother or father in the picture. I had no real home. People in those days generally stayed within their ethnic and religious groups. And it never occurred to me that girls who were only 15 years old weren't allowed to date. I had always been free to do whatever I wanted, but that freedom came at a price.

From Jeanne's 15th birthday to her 18th, her family made it difficult for us to see each other. I tried everything I could think of so we could have some time together, but it wasn't easy.

There were a few things that we still managed to do. Jeanne was allowed to go to the Saturday night dances at the ballroom in Waite Park. She would get on the city bus at 8:00 o'clock and I would catch it a few blocks later. We rode the bus to the end of the line and danced for hours. We danced every waltz and two step.

Afterwards I rode the bus with Jeanne as far as her house to say goodnight, and then would walk the mile back to where I lived. We danced all night and picked our favorite songs: "Three O'Clock in the Morning," "The Melody of Love," "The Waltz You Saved for Me," and "To Each His Own." I knew the words to these and to so many more. Every time we were together, I sang to Jeanne. She never once told me to shut up!

To Each His Own
(Made popular by The Ink Spots)

A rose must remain with the sun and the rain
Or its lovely promise won't come true

To each his own, to each his own
And my own is you

What good is a song if the words
just don't belong?

And a dream must be a dream for two
No good alone, to each his own

For me there's you

If a flame is to grow there must be a glow
To open each door there's a key

I need you, I know, I can't let you go
Your touch means too much to me

Two lips must insist on two more to be kissed
Or they'll never know what love can do

To each his own, I've found my own
One and only you.

That summer Jeanne was babysitting every day, plus worked at the Cafe. She got off at noon on Thursdays, but since her mother had put a stop to me seeing Jeanne, I rarely got to see her. We couldn't be together as often as I wanted and eventually it became nearly impossible. Jeanne had two years of school left and I was still working at the medical center.

I was learning a lot in the optical shop at the medical center. Although I was gaining valuable skills for the future, I needed money for the present. I asked for $25 for the 5 1/2 days I worked each week. They were slow in increasing my wages. By the time I did get an increase to $25, it was time for me to find out what the world would pay for an honest week's work.

Before winter set in, I wanted to go away to see what I could find in other parts of the country. I knew some guys who were seniors at Tech High School. They wanted to see what they could do after graduation. Everyone in my group was making about the same wages. My brother Gene found a job at a refrigerator factory making $35 a week. It looked like hard work to me. So when the guys graduated, Gene and I went with them to Chicago and Detroit. We had heard that during the war people could make a lot of money working in defense plants. We wanted to see if factories still paid good wages.

This was the first time that all of us except Gene had been away from home. Bill, Dennis and another fella were eager to get started on their adventure. We spent some time bumming around Chicago before heading to Detroit. The first day in Detroit the three guys found jobs for $75 a week. This was triple the amount you could make in St. Cloud. But I decided to go back home. My intention was to return to Detroit after I checked with Jeanne to see if there was a chance things could work out for us. It didn't look as if anything was going to change. Jeanne had two years of school left. Between that and her job at the Cafe and babysitting, there was little time left for me.

When I got home, I went to my boss at the optical shop and asked for a raise. I told them people were making $75 a week in Detroit. They said that no one could match those wages in St. Cloud. There were other benefits to living here, but none that made me want to stay.

Jeanne, the Angel Who Saved Me

CHAPTER 10

My Great Adventure

One of the saddest days of my life was when I could no longer see a way for Jeanne and me to be together anymore. She was busy with school and work. I wasn't going to get a raise. There was nothing left for me in this town. I packed a duffel bag with a change of clothes and a little less than a hundred dollars in my pocket. I was heading to California and the start of my "Great Adventure." I had always wanted to do a bit of traveling before I settled down in a new place and a new job. Now was the time to make a change.

For the next three years, whenever I wasn't working in the Detroit factories or they were closed for holidays, I took off. I traveled through 40 states and most of Canada, went to California six times, and went to Florida during one of the worst winters of the 20th Century. There were times that I got into some scary situations. All this time I had one goal in mind: to hang on until Jeanne was 18 years old and emancipated. I was counting the days until I could return to the Love of my Life and tell her I wanted to marry her.

Leaving St Cloud in 1947 I started out on the road south to Kansas City. I hitchhiked through Kansas and was picked up by a well-dressed man in a new car. He was very friendly and wanted to know all about me. We rode together to the center of the state and then he told me he was an FBI agent. He was checking me out. He was investigating a series of break-ins and burglaries along the road we were traveling. We wished each other luck, and then he gave me some information that I found useful over the next couple years. He told me there were Travel Bureaus in large cities where you could meet drivers who were. Traveling across country and needed someone to share the driving and expenses. It was safer for riders to travel with others you got to know before you got in the car. There was always someone going your way.

Late that night we stopped in a town called Colby, Kansas. The area was lit up and alive with partiers. It looked like a movie set of the Gold Rush Days. Oil had been discovered in the area and hundreds of people had come to work on the oil rigs.

On the road to Denver the next morning the driver I was riding with warned me about traveling through mountains. People would be reluctant to pick up strangers. It would be hard to get a ride. He dropped me off at his destination point and I headed out. After walking through the mountains all day, I found a ride to the airport. There I boarded a DC3, a very popular plane used during the war to transport paratroopers to Normandy. War was over and this was the first plane that the airlines started using for commercial travel. The first leg of our flight was to Cheyenne, Wyoming.

From my window in the airplane I could see mountains on both sides of us. I asked the stewardess how high we were flying. She said 11,000 feet. I knew that the mountain ranges reached 14,000 feet so I was curious how the pilot would manage that. I laughed when she answered, "He tries to fly between them." The mountain range through the Salt Lake Valley seemed never-ending. I looked forward to being back on the ground.

On the flight I met a man from Los Angeles who was stopping in Las Vegas for the night. He told me it would be difficult to find a ride from Vegas. He expected there would be a hundred people on the road to Los Angeles. From the air I could just make out a line of people extending all the way to the California line. I decided to take the train the rest of the way to the coast. The ride through the Mojave Desert was interesting but Los Angeles was not. The weather was always warm and sunny, but I was running out of money and I had to find a job. I had lost my duffel bag with my clothes in it when the truck I was riding in hit a bump and it flew out of the back. I had only the clothes on my back.

I took a bus to Long Beach and I stayed there until I was almost penniless. Decided to head east out of Long Beach thinking I could get to Detroit where I could likely find a job. I arrived at the Travel Bureau downtown. There was a man there who was looking for a driver to go to Denver. The man was a skip tracer who worked for a bank in Denver. His job was to find cars that the bank owned. People would make a down payment on a car, and then run away without paying the rest of the loan. I agreed to drive a car across the desert. There was no battery in this car. It ran off a generator. In order to drive the car at night the car had to be kept running. If the engine died, the car and driver would be stranded in the middle of the desert with no power and no lights.

When we got as far as Las Vegas, we got an order to go to Salt Lake City where we would pick up another car. We found the car in a driveway. We parked a block away to check out the best way to take possession of the vehicle. We agreed the easiest time would be at supper time when the neighborhood was quiet. The boss had a set of keys for every car the bank owned. I was told to watch closely and learn how to repossess a car. To anyone who was watching it looked like someone was stealing the car. We got away okay, but I was looking over my shoulder for an entire day to see if anybody was coming after us. We now had three cars. The boss towed the car without a battery, and I got to drive the brand new car. The car I drove was the first automatic transmission that I had ever driven. It took me some time to get used to it.

We took the road east to Evanston, Wyoming , and then across the state to Cheyenne, before heading south to Denver where we delivered the cars to the bank. The Repo-man asked me if I wanted to go to Albuquerque, New Mexico to pick up another car. I agreed and we headed south. We never did find that car. Next we were to head back to Los Angeles. I told the Repo-man that I was out of money. I liked driving around with him. It was interesting learning new ways to make a living. But I needed a job that would pay. He said he had to get the cars back to the bank as cheaply as possible. There wasn't any money to pay more than one driver. It was why the Travel Bureaus were a good solution for him.

We parted ways on Route 66. He turned west toward Los Angeles and I headed east toward Texas. In the Texas Panhandle I was picked up by a soldier who was going to Washington, D.C. He had a court date two days away. He said if I would help drive he would make it in time. He gave me some of his clothes to replace mine that I'd lost along the way. We both needed each other so it worked out.

In Illinois, it was raining hard when we hit a construction zone. The road narrowed down to one lane. It was impossible to see ahead more than a few feet. The driver took a chance and started out on the road. After a hundred feet, headlights of a truck came straight at us. The driver made a hard-right turn and we bounced along the side of trailer. The driver's side of the car was severely damaged. The car was still drivable, so we kept driving.

Detroit was only a 100 or so miles north of where we were. I told the soldier that I knew someone there and wanted to go to Detroit rather than with him all the way to Washington. I needed to earn some money. We wished each other well and went in different ways. I thought this would be the end of my travels. I had no idea what would be ahead for me.

David Sieben

Jeanne, the Angel Who Saved Me

CHAPTER 11

Working for Chrysler (1947–1949)

I spent the next two years working for Chrysler in Detroit. My first job was to supply nuts and bolts to each workstation along the assembly line. After a few weeks, the foreman promoted me to relief man. A relief man took over a coworker's job while they were on their 15 minute break. The union mandated that each worker take a break every two hours. There were six stations, ranging from assembling parts to installing brakes. While covering coworkers' breaks I became familiar with 30 different assemblies.

Soon I was promoted again to utility man, meaning I could work on all different kinds of units. The plant was a mile long. They put a car frame on the beginning of the line and hooked it up to a conveyor every four feet. There was a worker on both sides adding parts as the line moved along. At the end of the line the completed car was driven to the parking lot to be loaded onto a truck to be taken to car dealers all over the United States. Eventually, I was moved up once again to Hydraulics Tester. Whenever a unit wouldn't hold up under pressure or leaked hydraulic fluid, I would reject it and send it back for rebuild. The work came easy to me and I was earning 70 dollars a week, nearly three times what I was getting in St. Cloud at the medical center.

One day a guy from the front office came to my work station and said they needed my birth certificate in order to prove I was old enough to work in a dangerous environment. I agreed go back to where I was born and find a copy of my birth certificate over Christmas break. The factories were closed down for two weeks over Christmas so the workers could go home to be with their families. Most of the workers were from the southern states- a number from the hills of Appalachia. My coworkers called me the "pine tree hillbilly" since I was from Minnesota or "the Kid" because of my youth.

I boarded the New York Central train to Chicago and then the Rock Island Rail to Minneapolis. When I got to St. Cloud, I went to the county courthouse to inquire about a birth certificate. There was no record of my birth in the files of the courthouse. I then went to St. Paul's Church in Sauk Centre where I had lived as a child. The priest was no longer at St. Paul's, so I asked the housekeeper to get the records and write down the information recorded for the date I gave her. There was one word written in Latin and nothing else. I was told I had to get an affidavit from someone who was present at my birth who could vouch for me. I went to an aunt, a sister of my mother's who had never liked me, to ask if she would write a note stating she was present at my birth. This aunt never failed to get a dig in at me and often told me, "You're just like your father." After much pleading, my aunt wrote a note affirming she was present at my birth. I took the note to the courthouse where they made out a new birth certificate in red ink to indicate that the certificate had been changed.

For the rest of the Christmas break in St. Cloud, I visited with a few of the guys that I used to hang around with. I told them they could make a lot more money working in car factories in Detroit. I told them they were sure to get a job and make at least double what they were getting in St Cloud. I talked to Raymond Bares, whose mother had invited me to live with her family earlier. I convinced him to go to Detroit with me. We could drive back with one of the guys. He could live with me, work with me, and we could go to museums and movies. I wanted a quieter life than some of the other guys there who hung out at bars. There would be five more guys in Detroit to add to the three that were already there.

One night in the late 60s, I got a phone call from Minnesota saying that Raymond, his wife and daughter were killed in a car crash in Indiana. Although deeply saddened by the loss of this old friend, I was satisfied that I had had the chance to repay his family for the kindness his mother had shown me.

On our last night before we left to go back to Detroit, the guys wanted to go out and drink a few beers. We went to a tavern in the woods by the river in Waite Park. When the door opened, I saw Jeanne there with Richard, the guy her parents wanted her to marry when she was old enough. I watched until Richard got up to go to the bar to order another beer. When Jeanne was alone, I went up to her and asked her if she would write me back if I wrote her first. She said yes. We wrote each other once a week for the next two years. These letters Jeanne and I read together years later and burned them in our fireplace.

On the way back to Detroit with the_ guys, we drove through an ice storm. The roads were slippery. There was zero visibility. Fortunately, we arrived back to Detroit without any casualties. The factories all opened on time and all the new guys found jobs in the car factories.

Raymond moved in with me and worked only a few hundred feet away. He enrolled at Wayne University and sold encyclopedias on weekends. The two of us shared some of the same interests. We spent most of our free time together. We sometimes went to movies or to dances where we enjoyed big band music.

Work was going well and we worked all winter.

In May there was talk of the plant going on strike. All the Chrysler plants were closing. Raymond and I agreed to go on a trip to the east coast while the strike was on. I was the skilled one when it came to travel. I knew a man whose wife died recently and was going to Connecticut to grieve. He agreed to take the two of us with him. We ended up in Hartford, Connecticut. After wishing the man well, we went to church to pray for a safe and interesting journey.

We started out walking toward the Atlantic coast thinking that we would see the ocean first before heading to New York City. After a half day of walking , we decided the ocean was too far away. We hitched a ride to Long Island. From there we took a bus to Manhattan and toured the Empire State Building. While looking at the city from the top, I made a bucket list of things to do in my lifetime. I checked off the last item on my list when I went to Hawaii in 2016. Sadly, Jeanne was no longer with me.

Raymond and I completed the first thing on my bucket list by visiting Grand Central Station. We stayed there overnight, sleeping on benches with no interference from the police. After a couple days of sightseeing we went to New Jersey, and then Delaware and Maryland. In Washington, D.C. we saw the Washington Monument, the Capitol, and the Smithsonian Museums. The Smithsonian Museums stick in my memory most vividly. Twenty years later I returned to Washington, DC with Jeanne and our children to visit the remaining museums that I hadn't had time to see with Raymond .

Raymond and I were running out of cash after a few days, so we decided that it was time to head back to Detroit. We had a difficult time going through West Virginia because the people didn't trust strangers. All day Sunday we stood or sat alongside the highway. Nobody picked us up. When it was getting dark, a man who said he was in law enforcement advised us that people in the Appalachians were wary of strangers and would never pick up two people together. Raymond and I split up. We tossed a coin to see who would go first. I won the toss and was picked up shortly while Raymond stayed out of sight.

When I reached Ohio, I was picked up by a man heading to Los Angeles. I told him I lived and worked in Detroit and that the plant was on strike. The man had a car radio and we tuned in to a Detroit radio station. Apparently, the Chrysler strike was still on and it didn't look like it would be settled for at least a week. I got as far as Long Beach and decided to hang around there for a while. Raymond had not made it out to California, so I was on my own.

When I was ready to leave the beach, I went downtown to the Travel Bureau to see if anyone was going east. A man with a big car was going to St Louis and could take tour passengers. One of the men in the group said he was writing a book about people who moved around the country until they found what they were looking for. He invited each of us to tell him what was happening in our life. One man was going to the oil wells in Oklahoma. Two guys were going to join the grain harvest in the Texas Panhandle and stay with the combining crew all the way to Canada. When it was my turn, I told him that I worked at the car factory in Detroit and was seeing the country while the strike was going on. The writer told the other people that he didn't believe me. He thought I was running away from the law.

A few years later I heard about a book written by Jack Kerouac called, "On the Road." There was someone in the book that shared the same experiences as me. I think he was telling my story and that he wanted to dress it up a little by taking liberties with the facts.

While was on my trip to California, Raymond told me he had a hard time getting out of West Virginia. He returned to Detroit, and then went back to St. Cloud while the strike was on. He didn't know what had happened to me because I wasn't in Detroit when he got there.

When I got back to Detroit, there was a letter for me from my brother Donny. He said that when he graduated from high school, our Uncle Bill, the one who had taken him in when he young, wanted him to stay on the farm and work without wages. This seemed like an unfair proposal to me. Donny lived on a farm 50 miles from St. Cloud, very isolated from others. I showed up in St. Cloud and told my brother that he did not have to work for nothing. The days of slavery were over. I invited him to come to Detroit, live with me, and work at the factories where I worked. He could get 75 dollars a week. My aunt was unhappy that I took their free worker away. I said goodbye to Raymond who wanted to stay in St. Cloud to go to college and become a social worker. Donny took Raymond's place. We went to Detroit and worked for the next seven months without any layoffs. This was the first time that I'd spent any length of time with my younger brother.

Donny and I saved enough money to buy good cars. I got a 1937 Ford and Donny bought a 1941 Mercury. My other buddies all had cars now and we drove around every weekend. During the summer we made trips north to Lake Huron and stayed on the beach. The water was cold, but the air was clean without the smell of the factories. Daily we went to Belle Isle, an island in the middle of the Detroit River. On weekends we went to Pointe Pele in Canada on the North Shore of Lake Erie. We went drove to Niagara Falls once. On Saturday nights we danced at the Dance Hall in Windsor, Ontario at the foot of the tunnel. Every Saturday they had a big band play. There were a lot of young people to dance with. In Canada after the war there were many people from Europe because of the Open Door Policy. It allowed displace people to settle in Canada. I met people of different nationalities who had interesting stories to tell.

At Christmas Donny and I were invited for dinner at a house where there were twin girls. It went well and we felt better about being away from family. The Christmas break was on. I had agreed to go to Florida with a guy from the front office of the Chrysler plant. When we got back from Florida, Donny had gone back to Minnesota. Alone again, letters from Jeanne were all I had to keep me going.

Over the next year or two I made trips to Tennessee and Kentucky. I went to California. When I wasn't traveling across the country, friends and I drove to Toledo, Ohio to see one of the best big bands play. Two of the original guys I had moved to Detroit with had married. One left for Montana to build a dam. I began to think about my future and what I would like to do with my life. Working in the factory was enough money while we were actually working, but during the layoffs, there was no income and money got tight. By 1949, it was time to decide whether I wanted to continue at Chrysler or try something else. Jeanne was writing regularly, so I decided to go wish her a happy 18th birthday.

I bought a 1941 Pontiac that I thought would make a good impression with the people of Minnesota. I said goodbye to everyone, quit my job and headed north to the Upper Peninsula. I took the ferry boat across the lake. I went to Sioux Saint Marie on the border with Canada, then headed south to St. Cloud. I got to St. Cloud about 10:00 that night and knocked on Jeanne's door. I asked to speak with her. We talked a while. I asked her if she was available on her birthday. She told me she was going to a restaurant with her friend Janet and invited me to come along. I didn't know at the time that it would be the last day of my old life and the start of the rest of my life.

We met at the school, the St. Cloud Beauty Academy at noon and sat on a park bench by the river all afternoon. I told Jeanne I didn't want to be alone anymore. I wanted her to be beside me for the rest of my life. She said she wanted that too, but we had to get married first. I couldn't believe how easy this was when I was prepared to convince her. This is exactly what I wanted. We agree to first tell her mother and then see the priest. She also wanted to visit the lady she had babysat for since she was 15 years old.

On Jeanne's 18th birthday we went to Chef's Cafe where she had worked for years when going to school. This was the first time we sat together for a meal. Jane thought it was a good idea for us to get married and she offered to be our bridesmaid. Later we went to Jeanne's house and told her mother that we wanted to marry. Her mother told us no. She had promised Jeanne to someone else from a family they had known since Jeanne's birth. I said I wished she would agree to our marriage, but we both wanted this and we were going ahead with our plans.

I called the priest and set up a meeting for the following night. We went to see "Babe" where she babysat and told her the good news. She seemed happy for us. She asked me where I was staying. When I said I would find a room, she said she had a spare room and I was welcome to stay there. Jeanne looked uneasy about that and I didn't want to spoil our relationship the first day back. The lady had a life of many new men and Jeanne didn't want me to be tempted. I passed up the offer of a place to stay.

The next night we went to the priest at St. Anthony's and met not the man Jeanne had known since she was born, but a young priest just out of the seminary. He said it was sad that we didn't have the blessing of the family, but maybe their attitude would change as our wedding date got closer. We went to Raymond Bares' house to ask him to be my Best Man. His mother asked where I was living and I told her that I didn't have a place yet. Once again this kind lady offered me a place to stay with her family. I told her I would pay a dollar a day until I found a good job. I did find a job in construction. It was hard, dirty work. I was exhausted at the end of each day. Mrs. Bares said she had talked to someone who would hire me at an eyeglass factory making bifocals. I worked there for three months until our wedding .

I asked the priest if we could double up our classes and get married in three months instead of six. He assured me he would ask the bishop for a special ruling. The bishop agreed. Jeanne and I had intensive training in marriage and relationship. That religious training made a difference in how we lived throughout our married life together. Soon I would marry the Love of My Life.

I married the Love of My Life

Jeanne, the Angel Who Saved Me

CHAPTER 12

A Marriage Made in Heaven

On November 12, 1949, at 6:00 o'clock in the morning I married Jean Lesnick in St Cloud, Minnesota. Jeanne's brother Ollie rolled the white carpet from the steps of St Anthony's Church to the altar. The bride's father wasn't there to walk her down the aisle and her mother wasn't there to admire her new ring, a sad beginning for Jeanne's most important day. Her parents were teaching us a lesson. Jeanne's mother had already picked out her daughter's future husband, and that wasn't me.

My brother Donny drove around our wedding party after the ceremony. We went to visit some of my family who lived in neighboring towns. We made a few stops in locals bars before going to Jeanne's house. We found to our surprise that her mother had a· complete change of heart. She asked me if we would stay overnight. The roads were not safe. There was an early storm in November and there was still ice on the roads. I told Jeanne that her mother asked us to stay overnight on our wedding day and she said whatever I decided was what we would do. On our wedding night we spent the night just holding hands. I told my bride it was all right; we had our whole life ahead of us.

In the morning when we got up, Jeanne's mother met me when I left the bedroom, and said they were going to have a big dinner later. She asked me if we would stay for dinner. I told Jeanne what her mother had asked. Jeanne said again whatever I decided was what we would do. This was something we did for the rest of our life together. I always talked to Jeanne when we had something to decide and she would say it was up to me. Whatever I decided was the right thing to do.

We had our wedding dinner and said our goodbyes. We got out of town before dark. We intended to head south until we got to where there was no snow. We drove 50 miles to my brother Norman's house the first night. The second night we stayed at Winnebago, Nebraska, our first night alone on our honeymoon. The next day we spent the afternoon in Lincoln, Nebraska. We drove around the capital city and agreed that although it might be a nice place to live, we wanted to head south. It was already winter in Minnesota: all ice and snow. The flowers were still in full bloom in Nebraska, but would soon turn cold. For the last couple of years when I had traveled around the country, I came to the conclusion that I wanted to live where there was green grass all year round.

On our way south we stopped at Enid, Oklahoma to visit my friend Jerry and his wife Marge. They were the first of my friends to get married that summer. Jerry had joined the Army Air Force and was stationed there. They lived on the military base. We stayed with them for three days.

The next stop was Fort Worth, Texas. We checked into the honeymoon suite of the biggest hotel in the city. We stayed there for two weeks while I applied for a job at the Bomber Plant. The 8-36 was at the end of its run and the military was changing to jet aircraft. It would be some time before the plant was in production.

Jeanne and I went on to Dallas where I got a job with an optical company. Jeanne said she wanted to work, too. She found a job at the Baker Hotel downtown. She took the street car to work and got off at a grocery store located two blocks from our apartment. When the money we had was almost gone. Jeanne would use her tips to buy groceries. One month we didn't have enough money to pay the rent. Jeanne said she had some silver dollars she had saved since a child. We used 50 of those dollars to pay the rent. Jeanne saved the day by giving up something she prized very much. If at all possible, I loved her more for her unselfish act than I had before. Soon we were getting regular pay checks. Jeanne knew how to stretch a few dollars and we lived simply. It was hot in Dallas and we had no air conditioning. We had a fan that ran continuously. It wasn't all work and no play. We enjoyed going to movies and country music shows.

In our third month living in Dallas we thought that we were pregnant and she got a sit-down job as a cashier at the restaurant. We got a welcomed surprise visit from her mother and eight year old sister, Phyllis. This was the first time either of them had been out of the St. Cloud area. My mother-in-law said we would have a lot of babies because we always hung onto each other and were so close. She said that she could see we really loved each other and that I would take good care of her daughter That summer Jeanne's brother Ollie came to see us and then my brother Gene came to visit. I got a letter from my brother Donny who had joined the Air Force and was stationed at San Antonio, so we went there to visit him. That was to be our last trip before the baby was born.

On August 20, Jeanne's birthday, she wanted me to teach her how to drive. We went on a road that was lightly traveled so Jeanne could practice stopping and starting. After a series of jack rabbit starts the universal joint broke and I had to find a wrecker to pull the car into a garage. This was Sunday night and there were no places open. We had to leave the car west of Fort Worth and take Greyhound bus to Dallas. Jeanne rode in the wrecker. The ride was bumpy and Jeanne started having contractions. It was late and the street cars were not running. We had to walk two miles to the house we lived in and call the doctor. We went to the hospital immediately, barely making it in time. Our first baby, a little girl we named Linda, was born early in the morning the day after Jeanne's 19th birthday, August 21, 1950.

While Jeanne was resting, I went home and found that I had received a letter from the Draft Board directing me to report to an Induction Center. The Korean War had started and they were calling up the draft. I told the Draft Board I had dependents. They were not drafting anyone with dependents at that time. I was called up four more times that year and always excused. I never went to the Korean War.

For our first Christmas I bought Jeanne a sewing machine. The first thing she made was a cowboy shirt for me. I loved that shirt and was so proud to wear it, I wore it out.

*The cowboy shirt that Jeanne sewed
for me. I loved that shirt!*

Those Things Money Can't Buy

Al Goodhart / Ruth Poll
as recorded by Nat King Cole, Aug 29, 1947

To walk and talk with you in the moonlight, To share a kiss with
each star in the sky, To know you care for me only,
Those things money can't buy!

To have a one-way ticket to heaven Upon the wings of a dream
we can fly, To know I'll never be lonely,
Those things money can't buy!

To have a perfect understanding Is worth its weight in gold!
But dear, a perfect understanding You can't buy,
You know why, It ain't sold!

To have and hold you forever,
To know our love love love will not die,
To hear you whisper, "Darling, I love you!",
Those things money can't buy!

To have a perfect understanding Is worth its weight in gold!
But dear, a perfect understanding You can't buy,
You know why, It ain't sold!

To have and hold you for ever,
To know our love love love will not die,
To hear you whisper, "Darling, I love you!",
Those things money can't buy!

CHAPTER 13

All My Children

In 1951 we were happy living in Dallas with our little family. We thanked God every day for the life we shared. We hired a girl to help with the baby. Linda was uncomfortable and we had to drive around every night to help her fall asleep.

In the winter Jeanne's mother wrote and said her dad was sick. She wished we lived closer to Minnesota so we could visit once in awhile. I started to make inquiries to businesses north of Texas all the way to Minneapolis. I found an opening in Des Moines, Iowa. We packed up the car and headed north. On the way to Des Moines we stopped off in St. Cloud to visit Jeanne's family for a few days. By this time we were getting along well.

We were living in a trailer park just off the bus line. The new job did not go well. The manager was mean and dishonest. He was discovered stealing from the company. I did not want to be involved in anything dishonest, so we drove to Omaha for the weekend. A guy 1 knew from our time in Dallas was the new manager of an optical business He hired me and I accepted the job. I could use the skills I had developed while interning at the medical center in my youth. Plus, we could drive to St. Cloud in eight hours, so we relocated our home to Nebraska.

That summer, we found out we were pregnant for the second time. We decided that we needed more income, so I signed up for a class in police work. I went to night school while working at my day job making eye glasses for the optical company. The first things I learned in my class were CPR, lifesaving, criminal behavior, and conducting investigations.

We had been renting a place in Omaha. We heard of new houses being built in Council Bluffs, Iowa just across the Missouri River and within a short commute of my job. We bought a house with two bedrooms that cost about the same for our mortgage payments as our rent.

Child number two Juanita was born December 15, 1951 in Omaha. On the night she was born it snowed 20 inches. Our car was parked in a garage. The week before I had had an appendectomy and was unable to drive. Since I couldn't drive Jeanne to the hospital, I called a taxi in the middle of the night. We waited for two long hours for the taxi to arrive and made it to the hospital just in time.

My mother came to stay with us to help with our new baby. This was the first time she had been out of Minnesota and out on her own. She had been released from the mental hospital. The doctors believed there was a cure for manic depression. This wasn't the case. This time ended up just like the time in 1945 when there was a brief period of my mother's normalcy before the symptoms returned. The new drugs they had hoped would help did not work. My mother had to go back to the hospital. We went to Fergus Falls, Minnesota to visit her over the next few years.

In the spring of 1952, the Missouri River flooded. The business where I was employed closed during the emergency so I wasn't paid for two weeks. While the business was closed, I was still going to the police academy. We were tasked with helping to sandbag the levees on the river. I directed the big gravel trucks that were hauling sandbags. I was out for 12 hours a day and by the time I got home, I was too tired to play with my babies.

We had our first baby boy on February 22, 1953. We named him David. Soon after we were pregnant again and had another baby girl we named Barbara. She was born February 19, 1954, just shy of one year after David. Before Barb was a year old she got sick. After several visits to doctors who couldn't determine what was wrong, we found one who diagnosed Barb with meningitis. Jeanne and I put her in God's hands. We would rely on God's will for our child. Our whole world was praying along with us, and our prayers were answered. Our Barb recovered. We finally had our baby back.

Soon we found out that we were pregnant for the fifth time. On November 14, 1955, we were blessed with another baby boy and named him Dale. It was time to find a larger house. We started looking in Omaha, which would be closer to my job. The realtor saw us drive up in a 1948 Chevy and would only show us old houses that had plenty of rooms, but needed work. We wanted something new.

Jeanne's dad told us that he would take vacation time and come help us build onto our house. That summer we put on an addition: a big family room that was the center of our family life for the next eight years.

In 1958 Jeanne and I took a vacation by ourselves. We dropped kids off at Grandma's, and we drove up to Canada. Jeanne was only five months pregnant with our sixth baby. When we had gotten north of Lake Superior, Jeanne started having contractions. Knowing that having a baby this young would be disastrous, we cut our vacation short and drove at breakneck speed through Canada and northern Minnesota. We arrived at the hospital in St. Cloud where we saw the doctor who had previously told Jeanne she would never conceive because of a tipped uterus. This time he told her there was no doubt that she would lose the baby. He was wrong both times.

We stayed at Jeanne's mother's house where Jeanne remained in bed rest for three days. The doctor prescribed a drug for Jeanne to stop her contractions. We refused the drug, which was a good thing. The drug was Thalidomide, known later to causes severe birth defects. When her contractions stopped, we headed home. The kids sat on the floor so their mother could lie on the back sea packed in ice. We made a rest stop every 50 miles. The trip which would normally take eight hours took twelve. Linda and Juanita already knew enough about babies so they were a big help to their mother.

When we got back to Jeanne's doctor in Omaha, he told us that she had been lucky. Things were okay, but she should continue bed rest. Three months later, Dean was born seemingly healthy. He only weighed five pounds. We called him "Baby Dean" for the first nine years of his life. It wasn't until he took a school sports physical that they found Dean had a heart murmur. We lost Dean when he was 50 years old from a heart attack.

Three months after Dean's birth, we got a call saying Jeanne's dad was not going to make it. Jeanne took the train home with Dale and Dean. She spent most of her time in the hospital with her dad. She enrolled Dale in kindergarten for the duration her stay. I had the other four kids with me. They were well behaved. I had their mother to thank for that. Six weeks later I got the call. Jeanne's dad died on Good Friday. The funeral took place the day after Easter.

The bad news didn't end there. In July of 1960 I got a call that my sister Lorraine had terminal cancer. She died within three months. She left her husband Clarence with their four children. He couldn't handle it. One day he called his brother and asked him to come to the house before the kids came home. When his brother arrived, he found Clarence in bed with a rifle beside him. Clarence had never gotten over being in the World War II and his assignment as a sniper responsible for identifying and taking out enemy officers. Lorraine's children were taken in by Clarence's brother and his wife.

Despite all the sickness and death within our family, Jeanne and I were happy. We enjoyed our lite together. We had enough to be comfortable. Our children were healthy. We helped them grow and learn. But this wasn't the end of our family. We had more blessings on the way. With six children we needed a larger house for our growing family. We found a couple of houses that seemed to meet our needs. We wanted to be close to church and the school. But before we committed to a house that would be our home for the rest of our lives, we needed to make sure that this was where we wanted to settle.

In 1963 we went on vacation to California, making stops along the way. We checked for job openings. In Albuquerque, New Mexico I found an opening in an optical shop. I told the manager that I'd consider it. We drove on to San Diego where I was offered another job. The next stop was Pasadena where I got a third offer. We had a family conference to discuss our options. Jeanne and the kids said they would like to stay in Omaha.

When we returned to Omaha, we started looking in earnest for a bigger house. We found one in Northwest Omaha. It was the right house, but the wrong location. We wanted to live close to a church and parochial school. It would also be nice to have a grocery store and fast food restaurants within walking distance. We found a lot in Prairie Lane addition and placed a bid. I drew up plans for a ranch style house with four bedrooms on one floor. I took the plans around to builders. We found just the right one and signed a contract. They started building the house in September of 1963.

After President Kennedy was shot and killed, the market slowed and it became difficult to sell our house in Council Bluffs. It was listed in September and didn't sell until the following May. By Christmas our new house was completed. We moved in over winter break, leaving our house in Council Bluffs empty. Paying two heating bills in the Midwest cold winters cost us heavily. We put up partition walls in the basement making bedrooms for our boys. Upstairs, we put in a kitchen, recreation room and bedrooms for the girls. We installed a wood-burning fireplace that came in handy all winter. In the spring we added a stone patio on the south side of the house.

That June we went to Minnesota. While we were there, we got a phone call saying that there had been a storm in West

Omaha. It dropped eleven inches of rain. The creek flooded. People drowned. Our yard washed away. Windows were broken. The roof had to be replaced. Before repairs could be completed, I hurt my back. I took steroid shots and went to a chiropractor for months of therapy. Afterwards, I had surgery on my back to remove a disc. I was off of work for three months. This made it hard to pay the bills. Jeanne became an Avon representative. She saved the day once again. She became one of the most successful sales representatives in the area, and held this position for the next 50 years.

During this time I took the kids to St. Anne's and to work with me. In 1965 Mary Our Queen School was finished. We could all walk to church and school. Linda went to Mercy High School. I took her to school every day and picked her up after work.

Nine years after Dean was born we had another miracle. Maria made her appearance March 11, 1967. Maria lay on the floor beside me as I recovered from my back surgery. It was good to have a baby in the house again. We were really pleased when our blonde girl showed up. Now Jeanne had a mirror image of herself. I always enjoyed watching them and noticing how they reflected each other. It seemed like they were big sister and little sister. Maria grew up to be a very confident person just like her mother.

Between 1968 and 1972 we had five miscarriages. Doctors said the fetuses were not completely formed. It was nature's way of correcting itself. Jeanne and I were very sad to leave the hospital each time without a baby in our arms. Finally, on January 27, 1972 we had a healthy baby boy and named him Dennis. By this time Jeanne and I were both in our 40s.

The miracles just kept coming when we had another girl baby on September 1, 1973 and named her Diana. In 1976, we were pregnant again and our son Douglas was born on January 25th. We now had 10 children. I felt like Abraham of the Bible having babies so late in life. Every day we counted our blessings.

Jeanne, the Angel Who Saved Me

We cuddled each night. I told Jeanne I loved her every day and she did the same.

Jeanne was the best mother in the world. We had very capable girls to help us. Linda and Juanita took good care of the little ones when Jeanne and I were not there. Jeanne and I were very happy with our family. We helped the children with their school work and encouraged them to find something they liked to do, and then to pursue it through education.

We were delighted when Linda and Juanita chose to be nurses. When we built our new home in Prairie Lane in 1964, David, our oldest son who was in high school, was working at the Happy Hollow Golf Club where he took care of the locker room. He wanted to work and earn some spending money. He took care of the men golfers, cleaning their shoes and taking care of their possessions while they were golfing. David became the manager of the locker room.

While David was responsible for the operations at the club, he hired his brothers to help keep the place in order. Dale "Rocky" was in charge of linens and he did a lot of cleaning up in the restaurant and social areas. The next two boys, Dale and Dean, were also hired to caddy and work with people, many of whom were influential, well-to-do people. They worked at the club all the time that they were in high school. David and Dean both met young ladies there whom they married a few years later. Today David freelances helping people with handyman projects.

Maria found a job two blocks from our house at a Burger King. She received several awards for Employee of the Month. Maria also worked at the grocery store. She first wanted to be a physical therapist, but her heart was in accounting. She was so good with numbers. She studied accounting in school and went to work for a landscaping company and then as a forensic accountant for the FBI in Omaha.

We were surprised when Dennis didn't go the golf club route. He went to work for Burger King instead where Maria was working. Soon he surprised everyone by saying he wanted to be a nurse. After he finished high school, he worked for a traveling nurse company, traveling all over the country. Dennis went to Johns Hopkins University for a while. After 12 years he moved on the Stanford Medical Center on San Francisco Bay and ended up teaching medicine to student nurses at Stanford University. He found his love interest there and married a Chinese girl named Wen Wen. They have two children.

Barbara was always interested in everything in the world. When we went for walks around the neighborhood, she'd pick up rocks and study them. She would notice how they were all different. I marveled at her interest. Sometimes I thought I was looking at myself when I was trying to figure things out. Barb would say hello to everyone in a room, no matter how many were present. She always wanted to care for people. She took classes in gerontology and worked in old folks' home.

She wanted to work with mentally ill. Jeanne and I were proud of her for wanting to make a difference with her life. She spent many years of her life taking care of people at an institute for the mentally ill. When she retired, she continued to take care of people, working with refugees from Myanmar teaching English and life skills to children living in Omaha.

Our son Dale told us he wanted to study for the priesthood. He went to seminary in St. Paul, Minnesota. He did eight years in seminary. In the 1980s during his last year in the seminary, he went to Central America to live with the peasants in the mountains. On his team were a doctor, nurses, and social workers. Guatemala was in crisis. The United States had been giving arms to the police or the government there (Contras) who were oppressing the people. The government ended up killing 10,000 people in raids in the mountains. This was too much for Dale to handle.

When Rocky (we called Dale "Rocky") came home, he decided to take leave for a while. He felt the need to let people know what the government had been doing in Guatemala. He decided to go into politics. Rocky returned to St. Louis University where he lived with the Jesuits and studied psychology. He felt he had something to offer the world, even if he was presenting unpopular ideas. Jeanne always worried that his views would be challenged and bring him trouble.

Our family went to St. Louis several times to visit Rocky. All Jesuit universities have a community house where its students, priests, and families can stay. We brought in food, more than we needed for our own family, and Jeanne cooked. We kept the leftovers in the refrigerator where others could help themselves. It was always gone by the next morning.

Today Rocky is a psychologist in St. Louis, hosting seminars for doctors on how to rejuvenate and take care of themselves. Diana followed her siblings to Burger King, but wanted something different. She attended St Joseph High School for two years before the church closed it down. From there she went to Westside High School where she became interested in foreign travel. For her last year of college, Diana studied in Europe. She studied in Prague, the Czech Republic and a small place in Slovakia.

While in Europe, a group of her fellow students used to board a train every weekend. They traveled to the capitals of all the countries. They never had a problem other until the Russian border. There a Russian official said one of the students had a problem with his documents and refused him entry. The students voted not to continue on into the country if not all of them could go. This was a good example of solidarity in a foreign land.

While in Europe, Diana became engaged to Kelly Henderson. Jeanne and I were happy to see them together and were in favor of their decision to marry. Within the first year of marriage, they became pregnant and Kasia was born. She was not full term and had to stay in the NICU for many months. She had medical complications. She was diagnosed with Cerebral Palsy and needed skilled nursing daily. Her parents needed someone to be present when they went to work. They found a home three doors away from us, so we could be available every day to help with childcare.

Kasia needed to go to Children's Hospital every week for therapy. Jeanne and I took her for her sessions and then to Meyer-Monroe at the University of Nebraska campus. Each morning we would walk down the street to Diana's and Kelly's house as they were leaving to go downtown to work. We picked up Kasia from the school bus at three o'clock and brought her home. After getting her a snack, we played games, like watching the cars go by and keeping track of the colors. Kasia treated it like an arithmetic problem. When Kasia was born, we had an opportunity to relive our younger days taking care of babies again and it felt good.

Each Wednesday Mary Our Queen Church had religion study and we walked the kids to Parochial School for lessons. It was important to us that they learn about the church and God. When Kasia was about 12 years old, Kelly was offered a job in Washington state. We were sad when they moved away. We were so used to having kids around. About that time Jeanne was showing some behavior that wasn't quite normal, and we were concerned that we would lose her. I told my children that I would take care of her as long as possible.

From left to right: Diana, Douglas, Maria, Dennis, Barbara,
Dean, Juanita, Dale, Linda, David, Front: Jeanne and me

Jeanne, the Angel Who Saved Me

CHAPTER 14

Getting Away from It All

Jeanne and I were happy to see them together and were in favor of their decision to marry. Within the first year of marriage, they became pregnant and Kasia was born. She was not full term and had to stay in the NICU for many months. She had medical complications. She was diagnosed with Cerebral Palsy and needed skilled nursing daily. Her parents needed someone to be present when they went to work. They found a home three doors away from us, so we could be available every day to help with childcare.

Kasia needed to go to Children's Hospital every week for therapy. Jeanne and I took her for her sessions and then to Meyer-Monroe at the University of Nebraska campus. Each morning we would walk down the street to Diana's and Kelly's house as they were leaving to go downtown to work. We picked up Kasia from the school bus at three o'clock and brought her home. After getting her a snack, we played games, like watching the cars go by and keeping track of the colors. Kasia treated it like an arithmetic problem. When Kasia was born, we had an opportunity to relive our younger days taking care of babies again and it felt good.

Each Wednesday Mary Our Queen Church had religion study and we walked the kids to Parochial School for lessons. It was important to us that they learn about the church and God. When Kasia was about 12 years old, Kelly was offered a job in Washington state. We were sad when they moved away. We were so used to having kids around. About that time Jeanne was showing some behavior that wasn't quite normal, and we were concerned that we would lose her. I told my children that I would take care of her as long as possible.

Jeanne, still beautiful in her later years.

Jeanne, the Angel Who Saved Me

CHAPTER 15

Getting Away from It All

Around 2008 when the stock market was falling every day, Jeanne was having trouble remembering things in her life, like what day it was or keeping appointments to deliver Avon orders. When I retired from the optical business in 1992, I drove Jeanne wherever she had to go. We kept the Avon business going for as long as possible. This worked well for the first 15 years, but it was getting more difficult to keep up with the ordering, putting the orders together and getting them to the right people. I drove everywhere we had to go and Jeanne would go into the houses and visit with the ladies while delivering and getting new orders. Sometimes the ladies would call me and ask what is wrong with Jeanne- she isn't as sharp as she used to be. As time went by I had to do more with the Avon ordering and delivering.

Canasta was my wife's favorite game. For years she could beat everyone in the family. There came a time when she had trouble figuring out the rules of the game and sometimes the children would win.

Every other Friday I would drive Jeanne to the beauty shop and have her hair fixed. We always had an understanding that I would drive her every time she needed to go somewhere. One morning at six o'clock I got a phone call which said that Jeanne didn't keep her appointment at the beauty shop. I looked all around the house and couldn't find her. After about three hours she drove up to the house and didn't say where she had been or what had happened. The car looked alright from the outside, but then I discovered that the air bags had blown and there was damage under the car. Jeanne never did tell me what happened. Two days later we got a letter from the Department of Motor

Vehicles telling Jeanne to surrender her driver's license. Jeanne was with me when I handed it over and she was angry with me for a long time. That was the last time she drove a car.

From this time on she showed more signs there was something wrong. I decided to just watch her closely and take good care of her. I got a lot of phone calls from the Avon ladies who were concerned about Jeanne. I told them that I would take care of Jeanne and would have to close up the Avon business.

We were at a memorial service for our son Dean when Linda called to tell us we needed to go right home. She didn't say what was wrong. When we got home, fire trucks were there and our house was burning. The Fire Department told us that we had a windstorm, a downdraft like a tornado, that blew the hot coals from the fireplace onto the carpet which caught our house on fire.

From April until October we lived in a motel while our house was being rebuilt. We checked on the progress of repairs being done on our house every day. We built a new porch where I thought we could sit and watch the world go by. When the house was completed in October, we moved back home. Jeanne never could get back to where she was before. Jeanne would get out of bed in the middle of the night and stand looking out the windows. I could always get her back into bed and would hold her tightly until she fell asleep again. Sometimes I would wake up and couldn't find Jeanne anywhere in the house. All the doors were open and lights were on. I would go to the end of the driveway and see her standing on the corner. She was standing there as if she couldn't decide whether to cross the street or not. I watched until she decided to come back, then I would go back in the house and wait for her. If she came back to bed I never said anything. If not, I would try to talk her back into bed. These nights I hung onto her tighter than ever before.

There were a half dozen more times like this. We took her to Dr. Johnson who ordered an MRI and then put her on

Aricept. We knew what this meant. I decided to take care of her as long as possible. That's what I promised her the day we were married.

On May 14, 2009, I went to in the garage to clean the van and get ready for vacation. Jeanne followed me and hung onto me tight like when we were first married. If I was in the car cleaning, she wanted to sit inside too. When I opened the hood, she stood right in front of the car. I wanted to start the car and move her out of the way so I took her arm and walked her to the side of the driveway. Then I started the car while standing outside of it. The van had been sitting in the garage since last summer and when I started the engine, it rewed up like the accelerator was stuck wide open. The car started moving forward. I hung onto the steering wheel with my feet planted outside, and tried to get into the drivers seat.

In the next two seconds I had to make decisions that would change the rest of our lives. The car was headed right for Jeanne. I turned the wheel hard right and headed for the oak tree. The car hit the tree and I was thrown forward and hit the mirror with my head. I was carrying a phone with me, so I was able to call 911. The emergency crew arrived within a few minutes. I told them I thought my neck was broken. They put a brace on me and placed me on a board to go to the hospital. I think I screamed all the way, my back hurt so badly.

I did manage to turn the key off and not move until the emergency crew got here. The left side of my head was torn along with the skin from my forehead to my ear. The C1 and C2 neck vertebrae were broken off from the spine and numbers 6 and 7 were dislocated in my back. Before the day was over Jeanne was in another bed. We never slept together again.

I was in the hospital for more than a month. Jeanne came to see me a couple of times. I wore a neck brace for six months. Jeanne looked so sad to see me in that neck brace. We always sat on a couch and she tried to get closer to me. She would pat my arm and say, "My poor baby! I am so sorry!" and "Are you going to die?" This is how we spent our last four years together.

Six months after the accident I was involved in another crash on the corner by my house when the car I was in was hit from behind. The crash knocked loose the broken vertebrae in my back that were still healing. This time I had to have surgery with clamps inserted in my back and screws in my neck. During the next three years my neck never healed. I went to the neurologist often. He told me that this was as good as it was ever going to be. Today I get by with limited mobility. Back then I prayed that I would survive the car accidents and be with Jeanne until we both went to heaven.

From May 14 until Labor Day, Jeanne lived at an assisted living facility called Memory Cottage. When it failed to pass inspection, we moved her to another place called Angel's Touch, where she lived out the remainder of her life.

For Jeanne's last four years and four months, I visited her every morning at Angel's Touch. While I was there I also visited the other ladies in the home, all with memory problems. Sometimes the ladies would get confused and think that I was there to see them. I would tell them that Jeanne wouldn't like it if they saw me getting hugged by another woman. These ladies enjoyed music. I brought tapes of popular songs and played music the whole time I was there. It seemed that people with memory problems could always remember the songs they grew up with Jeanne always had a big hug for me. I told Jeanne I loved her every day for 60 years. Sometimes I think this was the best time of our lives. We never had a chance to be this close before we were married, so now we sat together with my arm around her and her head against my chest for five hours every day. She always tried to pull me in closer.

Only twice can I recall Jeanne not remembering me. She backed away from me when I tried to hug her. She said she didn't know who I was. I told her that I was her husband, the one who had chosen to spend the rest of our lives together. Every day Jeanne would run her hand across my face and call me, "My Precious." She should ask me, "Tell me the story about when we first met." This is when I decided to write our love story. I never got tired of telling her "our story". Sometimes I told her three times a day. I told her about when we had met, how we walked together every day holding hands. I sang the same songs we knew when we walked around St. Cloud years ago. She would look up into my eyes and say, "I love you, David."

About Christmas of 2012 the caregivers at Angel's Touch said it was time to put Jeanne in Hospice. There she would have more care from the nurses and health care workers in addition to the staff of the Alzheimer's unit. They told me that Jeanne was still alive because of me. I went every day to give her a reason to hang on. I was told by a nurse that Jeanne did not have more than two weeks left and I should prepare for the end. I didn't believe it. I thought Jeanne would be around a lot longer. One of our children would come to see their mother and take me home each night. I'd tell Jeanne, "Have a good evening and I will see you again in the morning." The nurses told me that Jeanne would repeat that she needed to go to bed early so she would be fresh and awake when I returned. That made me feel good.

About ten months went by before I got the bad news that Jeanne wouldn't make it past the weekend. At 8:00 am on the first Saturday in October 2013, I got up early and told my driver that I wanted to go see Jeanne. When I got there I was surprised to see our granddaughter Eve there with her mother Tiffany. Eve, who passed away when she was only 22, was sitting beside Jeanne and holding her the same way I always did, with her arm around Jeanne and Jeanne's head on her shoulder. Jeanne and I held hands the rest of that day. I told the caregivers that I wanted to sleep with my wife that night. I got that idea from "The Notebook" by Nicholas Sparks. The staff said they would make up the bed and make room for me. I crawled in with her in the afternoon and slept for an hour. My only regret is that I hadn't asked sooner.

Diana came in from Washington and all of our children that lived here came to see their mom. I called the priest, my friend Paul, and our family. All the people that Jeanne knew and loved were there for her last few hours. Paul started saying prayers and gave Communion to her. Jeanne used the last strength she had and tried to pull me closer to her. She was really trying to hang on a little longer. She had difficulty breathing so we got an eyedropper with morphine and put a couple of drops on her lips when she struggled. I told her it was alright to go now. We had a good life together and I would be seeing her soon. I told her that I loved her and that I always loved her and always will love her. I told her "Baby Dean" was waiting for her in heaven She couldn't talk but she formed the words "I Love You". These were the last words she said. A minute later she took her last breath. We were looking into each other's eyes and her heart stopped. Jeanne went to heaven about five o'clock that Saturday, October 5, 2013.

I thank God every day for the 64 years we had together. This was how I had always wanted our life together to end. I was the luckiest man in the world!

At her wake, I was surprised how many people showed up that we hadn't seen in years. The funeral was a beautiful service at Mary Our Queen Church. We always went camping every summer in the pine trees, so I picked out our last resting place under the pines at Resurrection Cemetery. Jeanne was laid to rest there. I have the grave next to her reserved for me. As we were together in life, we will be together in death.

Eternal rest grant to her O Lord, and let perpetual light shine upon her. May she rest in peace. Amen.

In Memory of
Jean E. Sieben

August 20, 1931 - October 5, 2013

Age 82. Born in Opole, MN. Preceded in death by a son, Dean. Survived by her husband of 63 years, David and children, Linda (Joseph) Schluter. Juanita Sieben, David, Jr. (Carol) Sieben, Barb (Timothy) Houlden, Dale "Rocky" (Ruth) Sieben, Maria (Jeff) Hamernik, Dennis Sieben, Diana (Kelly) Henderson, Doug Sieben; daughter in law, Barb Sieben, and many grandchildren and great grandchildren.

Visitation

Tuesday, October 08, 2013 6:00p.m. - 8:00p.m.
Crosby Burket Swanson Golden Funeral Chapel
11902 West Center Road, Omaha, Nebraska

Vigil Service

Tuesday, October 08, 2013 6:30p.m.
Crosby Burket Swanson Golden Funeral Chapel
11902 West Center Road, Omaha, Nebraska

Mass of Christian Burial
Wednesday, October 09, 201 10:00a.m.
Mary Our Queen Catholic Church
3405 South 118 Street, Omaha, Nebraska

Interment Resurrection Cemetery.

Memorial to Angel's Touch.

Apron Strings

Tie me to your apron strings;

I know there's room for me upon your knee.

Bring those happy hours

When you'd kiss my tears away

From day to day.

I thought that I was right,

But I was wrong.

Please take me back tonight

Where I belong,

Sing a cradle song to me and then,

Won't you

Tie me to your apron strings again?

David Sieben

Jeanne, the Angel Who Saved Me

CHAPTER 16

Grief and Bereavement

When Jeanne went to heaven on October 5, 2013, I felt I was alone and didn't know what to do with my life. I cried every night for the next three months. The VNA nurses formed a grief and bereavement group which I attended three times a week to see if I could get over the sadness I felt since I lost the love of my life. Everyone was encouraged to share their stories with the other people in the group. On Wednesdays, I would go to lunch with about 35 other people who had lost their mates. Most people wanted to share their life stories with someone who would listen and be available later when they were feeling sad. I sometimes stayed after the meetings and talked to some of the people who were having a difficult time and also called them on the phone to see if they needed to talk some more.

When I talked to some of the ladies, they shared some of the intimate moments of their lives and I was always glad I could listen and maybe help them with some of the difficulties that I had gone through. I was satisfied that I was well enough down the path to good health that I could help other people who were still struggling with the initial stages of grief. I offered others a sympathetic ear if they wanted to talk about their problems.

The most important thing I was doing for myself was to attend meetings of Celebrate Recovery. In the last years, I think I found the way back to being happy all the time. I have one special friend who took me where I needed to go and introduced me to people who would help me find the way back to good health. I needed to leave my bad memories in the past where they wouldn't bother me anymore. I am still working on my hurts, habits and hang-ups.

In my life now there is purpose and joy. I think I have found my life's work. I thank God every day that there is something that I can still do, things that can bring a smile to the faces I meet every day. I would like to be able to make other people laugh.

In my life now I still attend a Grief and Bereavement Group on Tuesdays and Recovery on Thursdays and Fridays. I now have a circle of friends that number

30. I have a friend who drives me to meetings and sometimes to restaurants. I feel that I've come a long way in the last years, and soon I hope to be in a place where I don't cry anymore and only have good memories. I have friends now who say they will help me get through the rough days. I look forward to the future more than going back to the past. It took me a year and a half to get to where I am now and I really look forward to the next year.

I believed that I had gone as far as I could with Grief and Bereavement. I now have a group called Celebrate Recovery that I attend twice a week. I've changed my outlook on life. I have a good friend who helps me through difficult days. I try to remember some of the good people in my life who helped get me through very difficult times.

CHAPTER 17

A Labor of Love

In February of 2014, just three months after my Jeanne went to heaven, I volunteered to help in the maternity, labor, and delivery and the Neonatal Intensive Care Unit (NICU) ward at a hospital. At the hospital my role was to be kind, compassionate and keep a calm and orderly place. As the gatekeeper, I welcomed pregnant ladies and their families to Labor and Delivery, and then escorted them through the locked doors to the room where they would deliver their babies. In the NICU nursery we had 32 rooms with all the equipment necessary to keep the fetus alive until they got up to five pounds and could survive.

Only the new mother and one other person could remain in "the birthing room." The others were invited to sit with me while we awaited news of the birth. I was able to visit with a lot of people about anything they cared to talk about. I have talked to a lot of grandmothers; some who would be grandmothers for the first time.

My first day was traumatizing. A lady came to the sibling area and stood just looking out the window. I asked if I could help her. She was looking forward to being a new grandmother but the baby died and she had to deal with her daughter now who was a rebel and very disrespectful to the family. The daughter blamed her parents for the bad choices she made the last few years and knew it was going to be hell when she returned in a couple of days to the home she rejected earlier. I could only offer my prayers and said when things looked their darkest, my wife and I put it into the hands of God and even the most seemingly hopeless things didn't seem so bad after a while.

I spent time with a lady who will never be a grandmother. Her 14 year old daughter who is her only child, lost the baby and could not have another. Another grandmother I had met was only 32 years old and expecting her daughter to deliver a child.

When my shift was over I went through the Labor and Delivery door and checked out for lunch. A young lady was standing by the door. At first she looked like my Jeanne. She was well dressed, blonde and her hair was put up like Jeanne's. From a little way off I noticed her name tag said, "Intern Chaplain". She looked like she was carrying the weight of the world on her shoulders. I asked if I could help her and she had a very difficult morning. She said I looked very sad and asked if I would tell her about my life. I warned her that I had just lost the "love of my life and that I still get very emotional when I talk about it.

At lunch time the young chaplain came by my desk and asked if I would go to lunch with her. I told her it was the best offer I had that day and I would be honored. When lunch was over and it was time to catch my ride to the library, she thanked me for what I shared with her and she said talking to me made her problems easier to accept. We agreed to meet for lunch every Thursday for the next six weeks. Talking to her was the most natural thing for me to do. I jokingly asked her five weeks later if her husband knew that she was having lunch with an elderly man every Thursday? She thought that was funny. It was part of her chosen profession to talk to people and find out what would make them more able to cope with life.

The next Thursday there was a note for me at the volunteer desk. It read that the chaplain would not be coming in on Thursday and that she had some personal business to take care of. On Easter I found a letter in my bedroom that was addressed to me, but no name for the author. By the time I got to the fourth paragraph I knew who the author was. It was a retelling of my first day at Labor and Delivery called "Just Another Day at the Office." The writing was much better than I could do. The events were told from the inside of the Labor and Delivery

Jeanne, the Angel Who Saved Me

room. When six weeks had passed, the lady stopped at my desk and asked If I would join her for lunch again. This was her last day as a chaplain. She was going to be ordained a Lutheran Minister the next day.

Jeanne, the Angel Who Saved Me

Just Another Day at the Office
By the Hospital Chaplain

This essay written by a hospital Chaplain describes her interaction with David in one day at the office.

Yesterday, March 27, was just another day at the office.

Except, my one hour commute was different because I had a passenger. My daughter, who chose to have surgery instead of enjoying spring break on a beach. A beautiful young woman who is hardworking, intelligent and compassionate. Who coddles the young and tends to the seniors. Who changes the diapers of both.

Yes, today might be just "another day at the office."

Except one of my greatest fears would be realized today. Fetal Demise—not one but two. From the first group session we attended on September 30th, I had dreaded the day that I would be called to the quiet end of the floor. As a mother of four healthy infants, I have never known the personal sorrow of a miscarriage. As a woman who was diagnosed with a hereditary blood disorder five years after I last gave birth, I now understand that I was high risk pregnancy. My life, and that of my children, was at risk. Fetal Demise would have been expected for me. And so, I carry a bit of quilt. Maybe it should have been me losing a baby but it wasn't.

Labor and Delivery...where I had just seen the "here we go again" attitude of a 30-something mother and father of faith who had just held and relinquished their 14 week fetus. Her second fetal demise in a year. Their child, who only yesterday, had represented hope, joy, and love...now lay still in a tiny blanket, hand crocheted by a volunteer. A child, whose arms and legs are no bigger than a cell phone charger cord, is now another reminder of dreams lost, grief

David Sieben

revisited and unanswered questions. How can I walk with these families when I have not felt their pain myself, although it was my due? No, this probably won't be just another day at the office.

Because...leaving those families, I met a man who seemed lost. The man who had earlier buzzed us into Labor and Delivery, was looking somewhat confused as I left after my second or many visits today". He said, "My wife is waiting for me," to which I intuitively responded, "But she' snot in the parking lot, is she?" With a sad smile, he told me, "No, she's in heaven." Funny how I had already known. I asked him to tell me about her, and he described first seeing the love of his life, who had died in his arms just five short months before. Now, he is a hospital volunteer. His role is to be a kind, compassionate, calming presence for the families awaiting news in Labor and Delivery. A lonely, lost, and intelligent man who had been searching for someone to talk to and thanked me for listening. Labor and Delivery, a place that was familiar to him, because this former orphan was the father of 15 children.

Identifying himself as a ward of the state after his father died and his mother was institutionalized for mental health conditions, this tall, once-athletic man had suffered. In many ways, his suffering mirrored the patients I had just left. Only 10 of his 15 children survived, the other 5 were what modern day medical staff would now refer to as "fetal demise." As we shared an elevator, a slow walk, and a pause at a crossroad in the hallway, we both ignored the curious look of doctors and nurses and visitors because we both needed more t1me together...me to hear his story...him to tell his story...and me to learn.

We now became focused on a mission...lunch. Where during the breaking of the bread, this Roman Catholic gentleman and soon-to-be-ordained Lutheran lady minister talked like old friends. Where he told of being a kid who ran away from foster home... repeatedly. And how the church was his salvation. Literally...and figuratively. As a boy of 16, who had been pegged a troublemaker, he had found shelter and acceptance singing in the church choir.

It was there that he first saw her, "the most beautiful girl I would ever know," looking at him. He was instantly smitten. The rebel was entranced by the girl who was already promised to another. And so, they fibbed to her parents… so they could be together, holding hands. Two young lovers, improvising because her mother was adamant that he, an orphan, wasn't cut from the right cloth and his roots didn't go deep enough. Finally, he left… to see the world and avoid the pain of seeing her with another boy. Leaving her with a gold locket containing his picture. Hoping she would hold it close to her heart.

And on her 18th birthday, he returned. And together they sat on a bench where they, with tender words, explained he didn't want to live his life without her, nor she without him. And it was decided, but not approved by her parents. Because he wasn't like them, with the connection of family or the foundation of a stable home. And so it was…her father didn't walk her down the aisle, her mother didn't hold her hand or gaze at her new ring, because they weren't there. Her parents told on their laurels and refused to attend the wedding. His parents dead or confined. But together they were joined, none the less, in a ceremony blessed by God.

When the new couple returned to pick up her suitcase, her mother insisted they stay. The roads were not safe. And their first night, as man and wife, was spent in her childhood bed, just holding hands. It was alright, he told her, "Because they had a whole lifetime ahead of them."

Now he spends his evenings writing his memoirs, and perhaps recalling that gold locket that held such meaning for a young couple. He sets aside his grief each Thursday, as he supports those who might be walking in his own shoes, as he too, puts in his "day at the office." I ask him if he likes movies, and he says, "I know which one you are going to say, *The Notebook*." Good guess. One of his twenty-five grandchildren had already given it to him.

But my day wasn't done yet.

Not everyone was sad in the waiting room. Sometimes there were disruptions that I would have to take care of. Once five young girls came to my desk and acted like they were having a party. I guessed that they were junior high students about 15 years old. I had to quiet them down or they would be kicked out of the hospital. One of the girls opened her coat and showed me her distended stomach. She told me that she was going to have a baby. I let her in to Labor and Delivery, but I told her that the other girls would have to stay in the waiting room and be quiet.

A young man came in and said his girlfriend was having a baby and asked where she was. I told him he could stay out with me or go sit with the noisy teenage girls who would probably be judgmental. He would not be allowed in the delivery room. I learned later in the day this baby did not survive. Another baby died before lunch making everyone sad all day.

When a family comes in with the new mother, if there are already children in the family, the birth of a new child goes smoothly and the children all look forward to taking turns holding and caring for their new little brother or sister. When the new mother is 15 or 16 years old, the future is not so bright. The girl is not yet mature enough to carry the baby full term. The baby may weigh only 1 1/2 to 2 pounds. Babies born at 23 to 28 weeks are put in the NICU and need a lot of special care. They usually need months' of care and the staff will make heroic efforts to get the baby to where it can survive on its own. When the baby reaches five pounds, if all vitals check out okay, the baby is ready to leave the hospital. The next part of its life is uncertain. After months of neonatal care, the baby will go home with the mother. If she has a family, they will help her care for the baby and make it possible for her to continue with school.

The NICU nursery was to the right of where my desk is and I talked to a couple mothers every day. The mothers would go home after birth, but the two pound babies had to stay sometimes for months after. Mothers came in every day to hold and feed their babies. A lot of babies were born in the 27th and 28th week of pregnancy, but once we had a baby born at 23 weeks that weighed 1 ½ pounds. I checked on this baby and he did well and gained a couple ounces within the first few days.

I remember a time when a very young lady in her 24th week came in early in the morning with contractions. The whole staff in Labor and Delivery tried very hard to delay the birth for a few more days in order to give the baby a better chance at life. When it was time for my shift to end, I really wanted to stay longer and see if the efforts that the staff was doing for the last five hours would be successful. When I had to catch my ride from the hospital, the issue was still in doubt. I prayed for a long time that one more baby would make it.

When I got home I had a phone call from a lady that I've been talking to for the last six months. She had issues that involved doctors, lawyers, a priest, and police, and court system, and family members who were addicted to drugs and stealing to supply their way of life. In the years, I talked to people who were recovering from the loss of their life companions and I am also learning to accept the loss in my life and put it into proper perspective so I can go on with what I need to do to gain heaven and spend eternity with the "Love of My Life."

I spent my days in Maternity and the ICU ward where I could be near babies who now have the best care. Every possible effort was made to keep the baby alive. This was nothing like it used to be when I was around the unwanted babies. These babies had a chance to survive. I was fulfilling a vow I made as a child when I visited the orphanage when I needed someone to give attention and care to. I always felt good about talking to these young ladies that had babies too young. I tell them that they have an opportunity to take care of one of God's Special Children. God chose them to care for his special babies.

My family stays close and talks and visit me every day. My volunteer work at the hospital was the most important thing I did until recently when I am no longer able to volunteer because of my health. I always look forward to the next time that I can talk to the young mothers. I applaud the decision they have made to deliver the baby even though their lives will be more difficult when the baby comes home.

Maternity was Jeanne's and my favorite place in the world and I feel blessed to be part of God's plan. I pray that I can spend the rest of my life being this close to where life begins. This is the fulfillment of a dream that has been with me since I can remember. I felt my wife's presence every day when I was at my desk welcoming new mothers and grandmothers. I know that Jeanne was smiling when she heard Brahms Lullaby.

I sometimes take an inventory of my life and see if I am accomplishing anything. When I met Jeanne, she told me of the corporal works of mercy. That had become an important part of my young life. When I had nothing, there wasn't anything that I could share with others; nothing of a monetary value. But I had an opportunity to spend time with a lot of God's children. When I think of what I didn't have, I can remember that I had the affection of children. When we visited with the kids at the Children's Home, I felt like Santa Claus. This was the most important thing that I was doing at this time. We worked with the children and knew that their day would be better because someone cared. To know one child could breathe easier because someone took the time to be with them. I will now work on adult people and try to win their respect. I hope to leave this world a better place than when I came into it.

I would like to know that at least one child has a better life because I have stopped to tell them that they matter.

Frank and me

David Sieben

Jeanne, the Angel Who Saved Me

CHAPTER 18

Volunteering with Adults

In August of 2015 Chuck, the manager of Volunteer Services in the Office on Aging, came to see me at my home. He said he had a request to help out a veteran of the Vietnam War. In the last 45 years since the war was over, Frank could not function fully or resume his life that was interrupted by the war. He joined the marines and went to Vietnam at 17 years old. He was severely traumatized by his war experiences and suffers from PTSD.

Up until one year ago, Frank would never could go out and meet people. He shut himself up in his room where he would sit in the dark. Chuck said he heard about what I was doing with mothers at the hospital and wanted to know if I would be willing to take on a grown man. This has never been tried before with someone who was severely affected by the war. I said yes, I would try and see if I could get through to him and maybe we could be friends. This was to be a pilot program to see what happened. I agreed to be a companion to Frank. He still visits me every week.

It was very slow going with Frank. He doesn't talk about his problems. We sit around a lot and watch television. Awhile, Chuck came to see me again and said a local television station, channel 7, heard about what we were doing and wanted to get this story out to the public to see if people would be interested in volunteering and helping to get a few more veterans to come in for help.

The television news came to me and wanted to interview me and tell a little about my role. On July 24, 2016, the story was on the evening news telling about how Frank and I are now buddies. He has a way to go yet. He can now talk to me about most things; but nothing about the war. We are going to keep trying.

My work at the hospital was still going well. The staff liked what I was doing with new mothers. The hospital had a banquet and gave me the 2016 Award for Compassion. There was another write up in the hospital newspaper. My supervisor told me that I was a celebrity and I got a hug every morning before 1 went to work. A lot of people came up to me and said they saw me on television and to keep up the good work. They said I gave the hospital a lot of publicity and they were proud to be a part of it. I am happy that I found my way in the world and a way of doing worthwhile work until I join the love of my life in heaven.

I began visiting the local library and writing up my story. While there I was able to meet more people and talk to them. I even ran into a young girl whom I had helped in the past. She told me what I had hoped for her. She went on to nursing school to be an Emergency Medical Technician because of my words of encouragement. It is always gratifying to me to hear that what I have tried to do makes a difference.

To the Love of My Life, Jeanne

by David Sieben

There was a time when I was gay and happy as can be,

But it seems like years and years have passed

since you belonged to me.

The smile you see is make believe;

It's really not my style.

But if you look close enough,

you'll see the tears behind the smile.

It isn't easy to pretend that life has been so sweet;

That Lady Luck has placed the things I wanted at my feet.

Where there's no love there is no life;

I've found it out by trial.

And if you look close enough,

you'll see the tears behind the smile.

Jeanne, the Angel Who Saved Me

Epilogue

When I look back over my life, these are the things I've learned. I have learned to be kind to people. "Love Thy Neighbor" has been my theme. Feed the hungry, clothe the naked, instruct the ignorant. Always help those with need.

One reason I went to the hospital to volunteer in the Labor and Delivery department is my desire to instruct. I remember how I needed somebody when I was young and that there was no one there for me to talk to- except for Mrs. Bares who offered me a place to live when I was homeless, the bakery lady who fed us from her day old pastries, her daughter who walked out to see me when I was sick, the head of Social Services for the County who took an interest in my future, the Chaplain who talked to me every day, and this precious 14 year old angel who told me about the corporal works of mercy. These people changed my life. I wanted more than anything to be that person for someone else.

I would like to be remembered as a person of intelligence, learning from my life experiences and from self study.

I would like to be remembered as a man of perseverance. Despite a beginning of few advantages, I struggled until I found the love of my life, fathered ten wonderful children, and accumulated enough finances to provide a comfortable home for myself.

I would like to leave my children with more than money. More than property. More than photos and this book. I want to leave them with good values, the desire to help others, and drive to be successful.

I am thankful for the struggles in my life because they taught me to be the person I am. I learned to be strong. I learned to be kind. I learned to love my neighbor.

David Sieben

Jeanne, the Angel Who Saved Me